THE INDIAN WAY OF LIFE

AN EXPLORATION OF THE PHILOSOPHY AND PRACTICES OF INDIAN CULTURE

DR. JAGADEESH PILLAI

Made with ♥ on the Notion Press Platform
www.notionpress.com

|| Dedicated to all wisdom seekers around the World ||

ഇ

Contents

Contents

Prayer

"Om Bhadram Karnebhih Shrunuyaama DevaahBhadram Pashyemaakshabhiryajatraah SthiraiirangaistushtuvaamsastanoobhihVyashema Devahitam YadaayuhSwasti Na Indro VridhashravaahSwasti Nah Pooshaa VishwavedaahSwasti Nastaarkshyo ArishtanemihSwasti No Brihaspatir DadhaatuOm Shantih, Shantih, Shantih"

The literal meaning of this mantra is: OM. O Gods! Let us hear auspicious words from our ears. O reverent Gods! Let us behold propitious visions from our eyes, let our organs and body be stable, healthy, and strong. Let us do that which is pleasing to the gods in the life span allotted to us. May Indra, inscribed in the scriptures, bring us fortune! May Pushan, the knower of the world, grant us prosperity! May Trakshya, who vanquishes enemies, bestow us with blessings! May Brihaspati bring us success!
OM Peace, Peace, Peace.

About The Author

Dr. Jagadeesh Pillai is a renowned Guinness World Record holder, writer, and researcher hailing from Varanasi, also known as the abode of Lord Shiva. With a Ph.D. in Vedic Science and a range of creative ideas and achievements, he is a true polymath. He is the author of more than 100 books including Research Publications. Although his roots can be traced back to Kerala, the people of Varanasi hold him in high regard and affectionately consider him one of their own.

In 1998, Dr. Pillai was offered a job at Banaras Hindu University, but he left the position after only two months to pursue greater goals in life. He believed that in order to study Indian scriptures and engage in other creative endeavours, he needed to retire from the daily grind of working solely for money at a young age.

He started an export business from scratch, using the knowledge he had gained from a previous job in the industry. His intelligence and unique approach to business led to great success in a short period of time, earning him more in just a decade and a half than he would have in a lifetime working in a government job. Upon the passing of Dr. APJ Abdul Kalam, Dr. Pillai decided to leave the business and dedicate himself to reading, studying, researching, and experimenting.

During his tenure in the export business, Dr. Pillai traveled to over 16 countries, gaining valuable insight and experiencing the world and life in detail.

Dr. Pillai has achieved four Guinness World Records in the following subjects:

"Script to Screen" - In this record, Dr. Pillai produced and directed an animation film within the shortest time possible, breaking the previous record set by Canadians. He has also received numerous national and international awards and recognitions for this achievement.

Longest Line of Postcards - For this record, Dr. Pillai created a line of 16,300 postcards on the occasion of the 163rd anniversary of Indian Postal Day. The event also included a questionnaire about the Indian flag.

Largest Poster Awareness Campaign - Dr. Pillai designed an awareness campaign on the subject of "Beti Bachao - Beti Padhao" (Save the Girl Child - Educate the Girl Child) to achieve this record.

Largest Envelope - In tribute to the Indian Prime Minister's "Make in India" initiative, Dr. Pillai created a 4000 square meter envelope using waste paper to achieve this record.

Attempted - **70000 Candles on a 210 kg Cake** - To celebrate the 70th Indian Independence Day, Dr. Pillai attempted to light 70,000 candles on a 210 kg cake, which was recorded in World Records India.

Attempted - **Documentary on Dhamek Stupa of Sarnath in 17 Languages** - Dr. Pillai attempted to create a documentary on the Dhamek Stupa of Sarnath, dubbing it in 17 different languages. The result of this attempt is currently awaiting confirmation from the Guinness World Records.

Dr. Pillai is skilled in teaching the Bhagavad Gita, a Hindu scripture, and is popular among young people. He has helped many young people improve their lives through his motivational teachings.

In addition to teaching, he has composed and sung numerous Sanskrit Bhajans and patriotic songs.

He has also written and directed several short films and documentaries for awareness campaigns, and has volunteered with the police in both UP and Kerala to spread awareness about various issues through videos and photography.

Incredibly, he has produced and directed over 100 documentaries about the city of Varanasi, all on his own.

He has also helped and guided more than 25 boys and girls to achieve world records through creative and innovative methods. He is a multifaceted person who uses his intellect and the blessings given to him by God to excel in various areas. He is both a teacher and a student, always learning and teaching, and is able to master any subject he comes across.

He is a selfless social activist and motivational speaker who has overcome struggles and failures to become a successful and enthusiastic individual with a rich life experience.

In addition to his work with the Bhagavad Gita, he is also an efficient Tarot card reader, Astro-Vastu consultant, and a talented singer and composer. He has sung the entire Ram Charita Manas and Bhagavad Gita in his own compositions, and has sung the phrase "Lokah Samastha Sukhino Bhavantu" in 50 different languages. He is currently working on a detailed and scientific study of Vedas, Upanishads, Puranas, and the Bhagavad Gita. He has also composed and sung the Hanuman Chalisa and Gayatri Mantra in 108 and 1008 different compositions, respectively.

Awards - Four Times Guinness World Records, Winner of Mahatma Gandhi Vishwa Shanti Puraskar, Mahatma Gandhi Global Peace Ambassador, Kashi Ratna Award, Dr. APJ Abdul Kalam Motivational Person of the Year 2017, Mother Teresa Award, Indira Gandhi Priyadarshini Award, Bharat Vikas Ratna Award, Udyog Ratna Award, Vigyan Prasar Award, Poorvanchal Ratn Samman.

Preface

India, the land of ancient wisdom and rich cultural heritage, has long been known for its diverse and multifaceted way of life. From its philosophy and spirituality, to its traditions and customs, the Indian way of life has captivated and inspired people across the world for centuries. The Indian culture is a rich tapestry woven from threads of spiritual beliefs, social customs, and artistic expressions, all of which are intricately woven together to form the unique fabric of India's rich heritage.

In this book, we delve into the heart of the Indian way of life and examine the various aspects that make up this vibrant culture. From the teachings of the ancient Vedas and Upanishads, to the central role of family, and from the celebration of festivals and food, to the rich tradition of music and dance, we explore the philosophy and practices that define the Indian way of life.

We will also examine the Indian caste system, the Indian education system, and the ongoing relevance of Indian culture in the modern world. Through a combination of historical analysis and personal insights, we aim to shed light on the intricate and complex web of beliefs and customs that form the foundation of Indian culture.

Our goal with this book is to provide a comprehensive and in-depth exploration of the Indian way of life, and to offer readers a deeper understanding and appreciation of this rich and diverse culture. Whether you are a student of Indian history and culture, or simply someone with a deep curiosity about the world, this book is designed to deepen your understanding of the philosophy and practices that have shaped India for thousands of years.

We hope that this book will serve as a valuable resource for anyone seeking to deepen their knowledge and appreciation of the Indian way of life, and that it will inspire a new generation of people to explore and embrace the rich cultural heritage of this remarkable country.

I

Introduction: Understanding Indian Culture

Indian culture is a rich tapestry of diverse traditions, beliefs, practices, customs, and values that have been woven together over thousands of years of history. It is a unique fusion of various elements, including religion, philosophy, art, architecture, literature, music, and dance, that have come together to form the distinct identity of India.

The roots of Indian culture can be traced back to the ancient civilization of the Indus Valley, which flourished between 3300 and 1300 BCE. Over the centuries, India has been shaped by the influence of various invasions, migrations, and cultural exchange, which have enriched its cultural heritage.

Religion has always played a central role in Indian culture, and the country is home to a diverse array of religious traditions, including Hinduism, Buddhism, Jainism, Sikhism, Islam, and Christianity. These religions have each contributed to the development of various philosophical and spiritual traditions, such as yoga, meditation, and the pursuit of self-realization, which have become integral parts of Indian culture.

One of the defining characteristics of Indian culture is its emphasis on hospitality and the importance of relationships. Family and community are highly valued, and hospitality is considered a duty and a sign of respect. Indian cuisine is another important aspect of the culture, with a wide variety of dishes and flavors, each reflecting the unique culinary traditions of the different regions of the country.

Art and architecture also play a significant role in Indian culture, with a long history of artistic expression, including sculptures, paintings, and textiles. The country is home to some of the world's most magnificent architectural marvels, such as the Taj Mahal, the Red Fort, and the Hampi ruins, which serve as testament to the rich heritage of Indian art and architecture.

Literature is another important aspect of Indian culture, with a long tradition of storytelling, poetry, and drama, dating back to the Vedas, the oldest texts in Hinduism, and the ancient epic poems, the Ramayana and the Mahabharata. Music and dance are also an integral part of Indian culture, with classical forms such as Bharatanatyam, Kathak, and Kuchipudi, as well as regional folk forms, adding to the vibrant musical landscape of the country.

Indian culture is a rich and diverse tapestry of beliefs, practices, and traditions that have been shaped by the country's long and rich history. It is a unique blend of religious, philosophical, artistic, and musical elements that have come together to form a distinct cultural identity. Understanding Indian culture is a journey of discovery and appreciation, revealing the depth and complexity of this ancient civilization.

"Indian culture is a rich tapestry of traditions, beliefs, and values that have shaped the nation for millennia."

ꟷ

II

The Philosophy of Indian Culture: Vedic and Upanishadic Thought

The foundation of Indian philosophy can be traced back to the Vedic period, between 1500 and 500 BCE, when the ancient scriptures known as the Vedas were written. The Vedas are a collection of hymns, prayers, and rituals that were passed down orally for generations before being recorded in written form. These texts form the basis of Hinduism, the dominant religion in India, and are considered sacred by millions of people around the world.

One of the central themes of the Vedic philosophy is the

concept of Brahman, the ultimate reality and source of all existence. The Vedas describe Brahman as being without qualities or attributes, beyond time and space, and eternal. They also state that the ultimate goal of human life is to attain union with Brahman, a state known as moksha or liberation.

The Upanishads, written between 800 and 500 BCE, build upon the ideas introduced in the Vedas and are considered the philosophical core of Hinduism. The Upanishads contain discussions on the nature of reality, the self, and the universe, and they challenge the traditional Vedic beliefs by positing that the individual self, or atman, is identical with the ultimate reality of Brahman.

One of the central teachings of the Upanishads is the concept of non-duality, the idea that the duality between the self and the universe is an illusion and that the true nature of reality is non-dual. The Upanishads state that ignorance of this truth is the root of all suffering, and that the goal of human life is to gain knowledge and realization of the unity between the self and the universe.

Another important concept introduced in the Upanishads is the idea of karma, the law of cause and effect, which states that every action has a corresponding effect and that a person's experiences in life are the result of their past actions. The Upanishads also introduce the idea of reincarnation, the belief that the soul is reborn after death and continues to be reborn until it attains liberation from the cycle of birth and death.

The Vedic and Upanishadic thought have been highly

influential in shaping Indian philosophy and culture, and their teachings continue to be studied and practiced by millions of people around the world. The concepts of non-duality, karma, and reincarnation have become central to the spiritual and philosophical practices of Hinduism and have also had a profound impact on Buddhism, Jainism, and other Indian religious traditions.

The Vedic and Upanishadic thought form the philosophical foundation of Indian culture, and their teachings have had a profound impact on the spiritual and philosophical practices of the country. The concepts of Brahman, non-duality, karma, and reincarnation continue to shape the cultural and religious landscape of India, and the study and practice of these teachings remains an important part of the Indian way of life.

"The Indian way of life is a holistic approach to living, where the mind, body, and spirit are intertwined."

ꟸ

III

The Bhagavad Gita and the Path of Karma Yoga

The Bhagavad Gita is one of the most famous and influential texts in Indian philosophy and culture. It is a 700-verse poem that is a part of the larger Hindu epic, the Mahabharata. The text is a conversation between the warrior prince Arjuna and the deity Krishna, and it is set on the battlefield of Kurukshetra just before the start of a great war.

The central theme of the Bhagavad Gita is the path of Karma Yoga, the practice of performing actions without attachment to their results. The text teaches that the ultimate goal of life is to attain liberation from the cycle of birth and death, and that this can be achieved by performing actions without being attached to their results. The Bhagavad Gita states that actions performed with a sense of duty, without attachment to their outcomes, will lead to spiritual growth and eventually to liberation.

The path of Karma Yoga is seen as a way to attain inner peace and liberation, and it is based on the idea that a person's actions have a profound impact on their spiritual growth. The text states that the goal of Karma Yoga is not to attain material success, but to cultivate a state of equanimity, inner peace, and contentment, regardless of the outcomes of one's actions.

The Bhagavad Gita also introduces the concept of action without desire, the idea that one should perform actions without any expectation of reward or benefit. The text states that performing actions without desire will lead to a state of inner peace and detachment, and will help to overcome the negative effects of actions performed with attachment to their results.

The Bhagavad Gita is a central text in Indian philosophy and culture, and its teachings on the path of Karma Yoga continue to be highly influential in shaping the spiritual and philosophical practices of India. The text provides a practical guide to performing actions without attachment to their results, and its teachings are seen as a way to attain inner peace, equanimity, and liberation. The Bhagavad Gita continues to be widely read and studied, and its message of selfless action and detachment remains an important part of the Indian way of life.

"The ancient philosophy of India teaches us to seek knowledge, wisdom, and inner peace."

ꕥ

IV

The Yoga Traditions of India

Yoga is a central practice in Indian philosophy and culture, and it has been a part of the Indian way of life for thousands of years. The word "yoga" comes from the Sanskrit word "yuj" which means "to unite" or "to yoke". It refers to the practice of uniting the individual self with the ultimate reality or the divine.

There are several different traditions of yoga in India, each with its own distinct philosophy, techniques, and practices. Some of the most well-known yoga traditions include:

Patanjali's Ashtanga Yoga: This tradition of yoga is based on the teachings of the ancient Indian sage Patanjali, who compiled the teachings of yoga into the Yoga Sutras. This tradition emphasizes the eight limbs of yoga, including ethical conduct, physical postures, breathing exercises, sensory control, concentration, meditation, and union with the divine.

Bhakti Yoga: This tradition of yoga emphasizes devotion and love for the divine. It is a path of devotion and self-surrender, and it involves singing the praises of the divine, meditation on the divine, and offering one's actions to the divine.

Jnana Yoga: This tradition of yoga emphasizes the path of knowledge and self-enquiry. It is a path of inquiry into the nature of the self and the ultimate reality, and it involves studying the scriptures and engaging in self-reflection and meditation.

Karma Yoga: This tradition of yoga emphasizes selfless action and detachment from the outcomes of one's actions. It is the path of action without attachment, and it involves performing actions without any expectation of reward or benefit.

Hatha Yoga: This tradition of yoga emphasizes physical postures and breathing exercises as a means to attain physical and mental well-being, and as a preparation for meditation and spiritual growth.

Each of these traditions of yoga has its own unique approach, but they all share the goal of attaining union with the ultimate reality or the divine. The practice of yoga is seen as a means of transforming the individual self, and of overcoming the limitations of the mind and the ego.

Yoga is a central practice in Indian philosophy and culture, and it has been a part of the Indian way of life for thousands of years. The different traditions of yoga offer a range of approaches to spiritual growth and self-transformation, and they all share the goal of attaining union with the ultimate reality or the divine. The practice of yoga continues to be widely practiced in India and around the world, and it remains an important part of the Indian way of life.

"The practice of yoga and meditation in India is a testament to the country's deep spiritual heritage."

ഌ

V

The Indian Epics: The Ramayana and The Mahabharata

The Ramayana and the Mahabharata are two of the most important and well-known epics in Indian literature. These ancient stories have been passed down through the generations and have had a profound influence on Indian culture, philosophy, and spirituality.

The Ramayana was written by the sage Valmiki, and it is considered to be one of the oldest epics in the world. It tells the story of Prince Rama and his quest to rescue his wife, Sita, from the demon king, Ravana. Along the way, Prince Rama is supported by a cast of divine and heroic figures, including the monkey king Hanuman and the god Rama himself. The Ramayana is a story of good vs. evil, love, and devotion, and it is widely regarded as a model for righteous living and selfless action.

The Mahabharata was written by the sage Vyasa, and it is considered to be one of the longest epics in the world. It tells the story of the Kuru dynasty and the great battle between the Pandavas and the Kauravas for control of the kingdom. The Mahabharata also contains the teachings of the Bhagavad Gita, which is considered to be one of the most important philosophical texts in Hinduism. The Mahabharata is a story of family, politics, and power, and it explores the themes of dharma, the importance of good action, and the consequences of unrighteous living.

These two epics have had a profound influence on Indian culture, and they are widely regarded as treasures of Indian literature and tradition. They are still widely read and performed in India, and they are considered to be sacred texts by many Hindus. The characters and stories from these epics continue to be popular in Indian art, literature, and popular culture, and they remain an important part of the Indian way of life.

The Ramayana and the Mahabharata are two of the most important epics in Indian literature, and they have had a profound influence on Indian culture, philosophy, and spirituality. These ancient stories are still widely read and performed in India, and they continue to be an important part of the Indian way of life. They are considered to be treasures of Indian tradition, and they offer a rich source of wisdom and guidance for those seeking to understand the philosophy and practices of Indian culture.

"The Indian caste system may have its flaws, but it also reflects the society's strong sense of community and shared responsibility."

ဢ

VI

The Indian Caste System and its Evolution

The caste system is a complex and controversial aspect of Indian culture and history. It is a social and religious hierarchy that has been a part of Indian society for thousands of years, and it continues to play a significant role in the lives of many Indians today.

The origins of the caste system are unclear, but it is believed to have developed in ancient India as a way of organizing society into distinct social and occupational groups. The four main castes, or varnas, were the Brahmins (priests and scholars), Kshatriyas (warriors and rulers), Vaishyas (merchants and traders), and Shudras (peasants and laborers). The Dalits, or "Untouchables," were considered to be outside of the caste system and were subject to widespread discrimination and oppression.

Over time, the caste system became more rigid and hierarchical, with strict rules about intermarriage and social interaction between different castes. The caste system was also closely tied to Hinduism, with each caste being associated with a specific duty, or dharma, in the Hindu social order.

In the modern era, the caste system has undergone significant change and evolution. The Indian constitution, which was established in 1950, formally abolished the caste system and prohibited discrimination on the basis of caste. The Indian government has also implemented numerous policies and programs aimed at improving the social and economic status of Dalits and other marginalized groups.

Despite these efforts, however, the caste system continues to persist in many parts of India, and discrimination and prejudice based on caste remains a significant problem. This has led to widespread criticism of the caste system and calls for further reforms and protections for marginalized groups.

The caste system is a complex and controversial aspect of Indian culture and history. It has evolved over time and has been the subject of significant change and reform in the modern era. Despite these efforts, the caste system continues to persist in many parts of India, and discrimination and prejudice based on caste remains a significant problem. It is an important aspect of Indian culture that continues to shape the lives of many Indians, and it is a topic of ongoing debate and discussion in Indian society.

"The Indian family is the backbone of the nation, fostering values of love, respect, and mutual support."

ꕥ

VII

The Role of Family in Indian culture

Family is an integral and highly valued aspect of Indian culture, and it plays a central role in the lives of most Indians. In India, the family is seen as the basic unit of society and is considered to be the foundation of social stability and continuity.

Traditionally, the Indian family is characterized by strong patriarchal structures, with the father or eldest male member of the family being the head of the household and the primary decision-maker. The mother is typically responsible for managing the household and caring for the children, while the father is seen as the provider and protector. The importance of family ties is also evident in the widespread practice of arranged marriages, which are still common in many parts of India. In an arranged marriage, the parents of the bride and groom play a significant role in choosing a suitable spouse for their children, and the family as a whole is seen as being responsible for the success of the marriage.

In addition to the immediate family, the extended family is also an important part of Indian culture. It is common for several generations of a family to live together, and elderly family members are often cared for and respected within the family. This close-knit family structure provides a strong support system for individuals and helps to foster a sense of community and belonging.

The family is also a significant source of cultural values and traditions, and it is common for families to pass down cultural practices, customs, and beliefs from one generation to the next. Family traditions play a significant role in shaping the cultural identity of individuals and are often associated with important life events, such as birth, marriage, and death.

Despite these strong family ties, the role of family in Indian culture is not without its challenges. In recent years, there has been a growing trend towards individualism and a shift away from traditional family structures, and this has led to changes in the way families interact and function. At the same time, however, the importance of family remains a central part of Indian culture, and it continues to play a significant role in shaping the lives of most Indians.

The family is an integral and highly valued aspect of Indian culture, and it plays a central role in the lives of most Indians. The close-knit family structure provides a strong support system for individuals and helps to foster a sense of community and belonging, while family traditions play a significant role in shaping the cultural identity of individuals. Despite the challenges and changes in family structures, the importance of family remains a central part of Indian culture and continues to shape the lives of most Indians.

"The vibrant festivals and celebrations in India bring people together and remind us of our cultural heritage."

ꕥ

VIII

The Indian Festivals and celebrations

Festivals and celebrations play a significant role in Indian culture, and they provide an opportunity for people to come together, express their joy and gratitude, and strengthen community bonds. India is a diverse country with a rich cultural heritage, and its festivals reflect this diversity, incorporating elements of religion, tradition, and regionalism.

One of the most widely celebrated festivals in India is Diwali, the festival of lights. This five-day festival marks the triumph of good over evil and is celebrated by millions of Hindus, Jains, and Sikhs across the country. The main day of Diwali is characterized by the lighting of diyas (small oil lamps) and fireworks, and the exchange of sweets and gifts with family and friends.

Another major festival in India is Holi, the festival of colors, which celebrates the arrival of spring and is famous for its playful and joyful celebration. During Holi, people throw colored powder and water at each other, sing and dance, and indulge in sweet treats and traditional foods.

Another significant festival in India is Navaratri, a nine-day festival dedicated to the Hindu goddess Durga. During Navaratri, people fast, perform puja (worship), and participate in traditional dances and music. The festival culminates in Dussehra, a celebration of the victory of good over evil, and is celebrated with great fervor across the country.

In addition to these widely celebrated festivals, there are also many regional festivals that are celebrated with great enthusiasm. For example, the harvest festival of Pongal is celebrated in South India, while the elephant festival of Thrissur Pooram is a famous festival in the state of Kerala.

Apart from religious festivals, India also celebrates several secular festivals and events, such as Republic Day, Independence Day, and Gandhi Jayanti, which commemorate important historical events and commemorate the country's leaders.

Festivals and celebrations play a significant role in Indian culture and provide an opportunity for people to come together, express their joy and gratitude, and strengthen community bonds. The diverse range of festivals in India, including religious and secular celebrations, reflects the country's rich cultural heritage and its commitment to preserving its traditions and customs. Whether it is the joyous celebration of Diwali, the playful festival of Holi, or the regional festivals, Indian festivals are an expression of the country's rich cultural traditions and its commitment to preserving its heritage.

"Indian food is not just sustenance, it's a celebration of life, a fusion of flavors, and a testament to the country's rich culinary tradition."

ꟾ

IX

Indian Food and Cooking traditions

Food plays an important role in Indian culture and is deeply intertwined with the country's social, religious, and economic traditions. Indian cuisine is known for its rich and diverse flavors, ingredients, and cooking methods, and it reflects the country's geography, climate, and cultural diversity.

One of the defining features of Indian cuisine is the use of spices and herbs, which are used not just to add flavor but also to promote good health and digestion. Spices such as cumin, coriander, turmeric, cardamom, and black pepper are commonly used in Indian cooking, and they are often blended together to create unique and complex flavor profiles.

Another important aspect of Indian cuisine is the use of vegetarian and non-vegetarian ingredients, and the country is known for its rich and varied vegetarian cuisine, which includes dishes such as dal (lentils), rice, vegetables, and breads. On the other hand, non-vegetarian cuisine includes dishes made with meat, poultry, and fish, and it is an important part of the food culture in many regions of the country, particularly in coastal and north-eastern India.

Indian cuisine also reflects regional differences, with each state having its own distinct culinary traditions and specialties. For example, the food of South India is characterized by the use of coconut, rice, and lentils, while the cuisine of North India is known for its rich and flavorful curries and biryanis.

Cooking is considered an art in India, and it is often passed down from generation to generation. Women, in particular, are the guardians of traditional cooking methods, and they play a vital role in preserving the country's culinary heritage. Cooking is also an expression of hospitality and generosity, and it is customary to offer food to guests and to share meals with family and friends.

Food and cooking play an important role in Indian culture and are deeply intertwined with the country's social, religious, and economic traditions. The rich and diverse flavors, ingredients, and cooking methods of Indian cuisine reflect the country's geography, climate, and cultural diversity, and they provide an insight into the country's rich and vibrant cultural heritage. Whether it is the aromatic spices and herbs, the delicious vegetarian and non-vegetarian dishes, or the regional specialties, Indian cuisine is an expression of the country's rich culinary heritage and its commitment to preserving its traditions and customs.

"The Indian education system has produced some of the world's greatest thinkers and innovators, inspiring future generations to pursue knowledge and wisdom."

ꕥ

X

The Indian Education system

The education system in India is one of the oldest in the world and has a rich cultural and historical heritage. The country has a strong emphasis on education, and it is considered a key factor in the development and progress of individuals and society as a whole.

The Indian education system can be divided into three main stages: primary, secondary, and higher education. Primary education is mandatory and free for children aged 6 to 14 years, and it covers a wide range of subjects, including mathematics, science, social studies, and language. Secondary education focuses on more specialized subjects and prepares students for higher education or vocational training. Higher education includes both academic and professional programs and covers a wide range of subjects, including engineering, medicine, law, and the arts.

The Indian education system has a strong emphasis on traditional subjects such as mathematics, science, and languages, and it also places a high value on practical skills, such as critical thinking, problem-solving, and innovation. The curriculum is designed to provide students with a broad and balanced education that prepares them for a range of careers and life experiences.

In addition to formal education, the Indian education system also places a strong emphasis on moral and ethical values, such as respect for elders, compassion for others, and a sense of responsibility to society. These values are considered an integral part of education and are taught through various means, including religious studies, cultural activities, and community service programs.

The Indian education system has faced several challenges in recent years, including a lack of resources, inadequate infrastructure, and a shortage of qualified teachers. Despite these challenges, the government has made significant investments in the education sector, and there have been notable improvements in access, quality, and outcomes in recent years.

The Indian education system is a rich and vibrant part of the country's cultural heritage, and it has a strong emphasis on traditional subjects, practical skills, and moral and ethical values. Despite the challenges, the government is making significant investments in the education sector, and there have been notable improvements in access, quality, and outcomes in recent years. The education system plays a vital role in the development and progress of individuals and society, and it provides students with the skills, knowledge, and values they need to thrive and succeed in an ever-changing world.

"The Indian sense of time is not just about the ticking of the clock, it's about living in the moment, embracing the present, and cherishing the past."

ꝏ

XI

The Indian Concept of Time

The concept of time in Indian culture is complex and multifaceted, with roots in both religious and philosophical traditions. In Indian thought, time is not seen as a linear progression of events, but as a cyclical, eternal process that transcends the physical world and is intimately connected to the divine.

In Hinduism, time is often described as a river that flows continuously, with no beginning and no end. The Hindu scriptures describe several different units of time, including the day, the year, and the eon. According to Hindu tradition, the universe goes through cycles of creation, preservation, and destruction, with each cycle lasting millions of years.

In Indian philosophy, time is also seen as an integral part of the concept of karma. According to this belief, the actions of individuals in the present shape their destiny in the future, and the cycle of birth and rebirth is driven by the accumulation of karma over time.

The Indian concept of time is also reflected in the country's calendar system, which is based on the movement of the sun and the moon. The Indian calendar is called the Hindu calendar and it is divided into 12 months, with each month having either 29 or 30 days. The calendar also takes into account the position of the sun and the moon, and it incorporates astronomical observations and calculations to determine the timing of festivals and other important events.

The Indian concept of time is also evident in the country's cultural and spiritual practices. For example, the practice of yoga is seen as a way of transcending the limitations of time and space and connecting with the divine. Meditation and other spiritual practices are also used to help individuals achieve a deeper understanding of the nature of time and their place within it.

The Indian concept of time is a rich and complex aspect of the country's cultural heritage, and it is deeply connected to religious and philosophical traditions. Time is seen as a cyclical, eternal process that transcends the physical world and is intimately connected to the divine. The Indian calendar, cultural and spiritual practices, and beliefs about karma all reflect this unique and nuanced understanding of time.

"The Indian aesthetic is a celebration of the beauty of life, showcasing the country's rich artistic heritage and inspiring future generations."

ꕥ

XII

The Indian Sense of Beauty and Aesthetics

The Indian sense of beauty and aesthetics is a unique and intricate aspect of the country's rich cultural heritage. From intricate temple architecture to vivid paintings and intricate textiles, Indian art and design is characterized by a love of intricate details, vivid colors, and symbolic meaning.

In Hinduism, beauty is seen as a manifestation of the divine, and art and architecture are considered to be a way of expressing devotion and connecting with the divine. The design of Hindu temples, for example, often incorporates intricate carvings, sculptures, and paintings that tell stories from Hindu mythology. These works of art are not just seen as beautiful, but also as a means of communicating religious teachings and inspiring spiritual devotion.

In Indian classical dance, such as Bharatanatyam, Kathak, and Kuchipudi, the graceful movements of the dancers and the intricate costumes and jewelry are seen as beautiful expressions of the divine. Music, too, is an important part of Indian aesthetics, with classical forms such as Carnatic and Hindustani music valued for their intricate rhythms, melodies, and emotional depth.

The Indian sense of beauty is also reflected in the country's textiles, which are characterized by intricate patterns, bold colors, and a love of detail. From delicate silk sarees to intricate weaving patterns, Indian textiles are prized for their beauty and their ability to express cultural heritage and personal style.

Indian aesthetics are also reflected in the country's food, with a focus on creating balanced and visually appealing dishes that are full of flavor and nutrition. Spices and herbs play an important role in Indian cooking, with each dish carefully crafted to create a unique combination of flavors, textures, and aromas.

The Indian sense of beauty and aesthetics is an integral part of the country's cultural heritage, and it is expressed in a wide range of art forms, including architecture, dance, music, textiles, and food. Whether through intricate carvings, graceful dance movements, or the careful blending of spices, the Indian sense of beauty is a celebration of life and a connection to the divine.

"Indian classical music and dance are not just entertainment, they are a means of exploring the soul and expressing the deepest human emotions."

ଌ

XIII

Indian Classical Music and Dance

Indian classical music and dance are two of the oldest and richest cultural traditions in the world. Both forms of expression have been passed down from generation to generation for thousands of years, and they are deeply intertwined with the religious, philosophical, and social fabric of Indian culture.

Classical music in India is divided into two main styles, Carnatic music and Hindustani music. Carnatic music is the classical music of South India and is characterized by its use of complex rhythms, intricate melodies, and a focus on devotional themes. Hindustani music, on the other hand, is the classical music of North India and is known for its improvisational style, use of intricate ornamentation, and emotional expressiveness.

Classical Indian dance is also diverse, with a number of

different styles including Bharatanatyam, Kathak, Kuchipudi, and Manipuri. These dances are characterized by intricate footwork, graceful hand movements, and expressions that convey emotions and tell stories.

In both music and dance, the concept of "rasa" is central. Rasa refers to the emotional essence or flavor of a performance, and it is considered to be one of the most important aspects of classical Indian art. The goal of a performance is to evoke a particular rasa in the audience, be it delight, wonder, sorrow, or any of the other eight emotions that are considered to be the building blocks of Indian classical art.

Music and dance have always been integral to Hindu religious ceremonies and festivals, and they continue to play an important role in Indian cultural life. From the elaborate performances held at temple festivals to the informal gatherings of friends and family, music and dance are a way of expressing joy, devotion, and the deep cultural roots of the Indian people.

In recent years, Indian classical music and dance have gained recognition and popularity around the world. The internet and other technological advances have made it easier for people to learn about and appreciate these rich cultural traditions, and there is now a thriving global community of musicians and dancers who are dedicated to preserving and promoting Indian classical art forms.

Indian classical music and dance are an essential part of the country's cultural heritage, reflecting the complex and rich history of India. Whether in the context of religious ceremonies or as standalone art forms, they continue to captivate audiences with their intricate rhythms, graceful movements, and emotional expressiveness.

"Indian cinema and popular culture reflect the hopes, dreams, and aspirations of the people, showcasing the country's rich cultural heritage."

ഇ

XIV

Indian Cinema and Popular Culture

The Indian film industry, also known as Bollywood, is one of the largest film industries in the world. The Indian cinema has a rich history dating back to the early 1900s and has evolved into a dynamic and diverse art form that reflects the cultural, social and political fabric of India. In this chapter, we will explore the role of Indian cinema and popular culture in shaping and reflecting the Indian way of life.

Evolution of Indian Cinema

The early days of Indian cinema were marked by the production of silent films, which were mostly adaptations of plays or stories from Indian mythology and folklore. With the advent of sound in the 1930s, the Indian film industry started producing musicals, known as "masala" films, which combined elements of drama, romance, and song and dance. Over the years, Indian cinema has undergone several transformations, with the introduction of new genres and themes, such as social dramas, action films, and romantic comedies.

The Golden Age of Indian Cinema

The 1950s and 1960s are considered the golden age of Indian cinema, marked by the emergence of several talented filmmakers, actors, and musicians who brought a new level of artistry and sophistication to the industry. During this period, Indian cinema produced some of its most iconic and memorable films, such as "Pyaasa", "Awaara" and "Shree 420", which dealt with themes of social justice, poverty, and corruption. This era also saw the rise of several legendary actors, such as Raj Kapoor, Dilip Kumar, and Dev Anand, who continue to be celebrated and remembered even today.

The New Wave of Indian Cinema

In the 1990s, Indian cinema experienced a new wave of creativity and experimentation, marked by the emergence of a new generation of filmmakers and actors who brought a fresh perspective to the industry. This period saw the rise of several critically acclaimed and commercially successful films, such as "Dil Chahta Hai", "Lagaan", and "Rang De Basanti", which tackled complex social and political issues in a bold and innovative manner.

Indian Popular Culture

Indian popular culture is a rich and diverse tapestry of music, dance, fashion, food, and more. From the vibrant and energetic Bhangra and Bollywood dance styles to the intricate and ornate designs of Indian textiles and jewelry, Indian popular culture reflects the country's rich cultural heritage and celebrates its diversity.

Indian Music and Dance

Music and dance have been an integral part of Indian culture for centuries, and they continue to play a major role in Indian popular culture. Indian classical music, with its intricate rhythms and melodic patterns, has a rich history dating back to ancient times, and it continues to be widely enjoyed and appreciated today. Indian classical dance forms, such as Bharatanatyam, Kathak, and Kuchipudi, are characterized by their intricate hand gestures, expressive eye movements, and graceful footwork, and they continue to be popular and widely performed across the country.

Indian Fashion and Beauty

Indian fashion and beauty are renowned for their intricate designs, bold colors, and elaborate embellishments. From the vibrant sarees and elegant Kurtas to the elaborate jewelry and elaborate hairstyles, Indian fashion and beauty reflect the country's rich cultural heritage and celebrate its diversity.

Indian cinema and popular culture are an integral part of the Indian way of life and play a major role in shaping and reflecting the cultural, social, and political fabric of the country. Whether through the imaginative and thought-provoking films produced by Bollywood, the regional film industries, or the various music and dance styles, Indian cinema and popular culture showcase the richness and diversity of the Indian culture.

These forms of expression serve as a platform for people to connect with each other and with their roots, while also presenting India to the rest of the world. In recent years, Indian cinema and popular culture have been gaining recognition globally and are contributing to the growth and promotion of the Indian cultural heritage. As such, the Indian way of life is not just about the philosophy and practices that have been passed down for generations, but also about the evolving and dynamic expressions of these traditions in the modern world.

"The ongoing relevance and significance of Indian culture lies in its ability to adapt, evolve, and remain relevant in an ever-changing world."

ജ

XV

The ongoing Relevance and Significance of Indian Culture in the Modern World

Indian culture has been shaped and influenced by thousands of years of history, religion, philosophy, and tradition. Despite being one of the oldest civilizations in the world, Indian culture remains vibrant and relevant in the modern world. In this chapter, we will explore the ongoing significance of Indian culture and its relevance in the 21st century.

The Rich Heritage of Indian Culture

Indian culture is renowned for its rich heritage and diversity. From the ancient Vedic scriptures to the bustling cities of modern India, the country's cultural traditions have been passed down from generation to generation. India's cultural heritage is reflected in its art, music, dance, literature, and philosophy, among many other things. The country's rich history is also evident in its monuments, temples, and architectural structures, which serve as a testament to its cultural legacy.

The Importance of Indian Philosophy in the Modern World

Indian philosophy has had a profound impact on the world and continues to be a source of inspiration for many people today. The ancient Indian scriptures, such as the Vedas, the Upanishads, and the Bhagavad Gita, contain timeless wisdom that is still relevant in the modern world. These texts offer insights into the nature of reality, the meaning of life, and the path to enlightenment. The teachings of Indian philosophers such as Patanjali, who wrote the Yoga Sutras, and Buddha, who founded the Buddhist tradition, continue to be widely studied and practiced today.

The Relevance of Indian Traditions and Festivals

Indian traditions and festivals are an integral part of the country's cultural heritage. From Diwali, the festival of lights, to Holi, the festival of colors, Indian festivals are celebrated with great enthusiasm and joy. These festivals not only bring people together but also provide an opportunity to preserve and celebrate the country's cultural heritage. In recent years, Indian festivals have gained popularity around the world, with people of Indian descent and others celebrating them in their own countries.

The Influence of Indian Culture on the World

Indian culture has had a profound impact on the world and continues to do so. The practice of yoga, for example, which originated in India, has gained widespread popularity around the world and is now recognized as a form of exercise and meditation. Indian classical dance forms, such as Bharatanatyam and Kathak, have also gained recognition and popularity around the world. Indian cuisine, with its diverse and flavorful dishes, has also gained popularity globally and has become one of the most popular types of cuisine in the world.

The Vitality of Indian Culture in the Modern World

Despite the many challenges faced by India in the modern world, its cultural heritage remains vibrant and relevant. The rich history and traditions of India continue to inspire and inform people around the world. The ongoing significance of Indian culture lies in its ability to adapt and evolve while still retaining its core values and beliefs. As the world becomes more interconnected and globalized, it is more important than ever to appreciate and celebrate the diversity of cultures that exist in the world. In this way, Indian culture will continue to play a vital role in shaping the world of the future.

"The Indian way of life is not just a philosophy, it's a way of living, a way of being, and a way of seeing the world."

ℵ

Other Books Of The Author

1. The Moments When I Met God
2. Kashiyile Theertha Pathangal
3. GURU GYAN VANI
4. Abhiprerak Gita
5. ASSI SE JAIN GHAT TAK
6. Hopelessness of Arjuna
7. The Soul and It's True Nature
8. Sense of Action (Karma)
9. Action through Wisdom
10. Action through Wisdom
11. THEORY AND PRACTICAL OF EVERY ACTION
12. LOGICAL UNDERSTANDING OF THE SUPREME
13. THE IMPERISHABLE SUPREME
14. Yatra Nishadraj se Hanuman Ghat Tak
15. Yatra Karnatak Ghat se Raja Ghat Tak
16. Yatra Pandey Ghat se Prayagraj Ghat Tak
17. Yatra Ranjendra Prasad Ghat se Dattatreya Ghat Tak
18. YaatraSindhiya Ghat se Gwaliar Ghat Tak
19. Yatra Mangala Gauri Ghat se Hanuman Gadhi Ghat Tak
20. Yatra Gaay Ghat Se Nishad Ghat Tak
21. MAA GANGA, GHATEN EVM UTSAV
22. Ganga Arti Dev Deepavali evam Any Utsav
23. Potentials of Digitalized India
24. VEDIC CONSCIOUSNESS
25. A Brief Introduction to Vedic Science
26. Kashi ke Barah Jyotirling
27. IMPACT OF MOTIVATION
28. Let's have a Milky Way Journey
29. Color Therapy in a Nutshell

30. Rigveda in a Nutshell
31. Yajurveda in a Nutshell
32. Samveda in a Nutshell
33. Atharva Veda in a Nutshell
34. Ayushman Bhava - Ayurveda
35. Srimad Bhagavad Gita and Upanishad Connection
36. Srimad Bhagavad Gita - an attempt to summarize each chapter.
37. Facts and Impact of Nakshatra
38. Astro Gems - NAVARATNA
39. Ekadashi - A Concise Overview
40. A Concise View of Hanuman Chalisa
41. Inspirational Gita
42. Nakshatraranyam
43. Summary of 18 Mahapuranas
44. Synopsis of 18 Upa Puranas
45. Rigvediya Upanishads
46. Shukla Yajurvediya Upanishads
47. Krishna Yajurvediya Upanishads
48. Samavediya Upanishads
49. Atharvavediya Upanishads
50. The Seven Great Sages
51. From Rocket Scientist to President Dr. APJ Abdul Kalam
52. The Visionary's Voice - Quotes of Dr. APJ Abdul Kalam
53. The Wisdom of Swami Vivekananda: Insights and Inspiration from a Legendary Spiritual Teacher
54. Ayurvedic Remedies from the Garden
55. Sages and Seers
56. Rising Strong – Motivational Stories of Women
57. Beyond Flames -Mystery stories of Funeral Ghat Manikarnika
58. The Origins of Tulsi: A Look at the Mythological Roots of the Plant"

59. The Holistic Cow: A Look at the Physical, Spiritual, and Cultural Importance of Cows in India
60. Arts of Healing
61. Exploring the Divine
62. Understanding Five Elements
63. The Etymology of Ram
64. Symbols of India
65. Voice of Change (About Speeches of Great Men)
66. She Speaks (About Speeches of Great Women)
67. Patriotism on Celluloid – Brief About Patriotic Films
68. The Music of Motivation: A Brief Guide to Inspirational Film Songs
69. **Unlocking the Secrets of the Dashopanishads**
70. A Cultural Mosaic
71. Ancient Traditions, Modern Minds
72. Ecos of Ancient Wisdom
73. Beneath the Surface
74. From Temples to Ashrams
75. Sages of the Subcontinent
76. The Art of Healling (Ayurveda, Yoga & Naturopathy)
77. Indian Kitchen
78. The Festivals of India
79. The Indian Epics Retold
80. The Power of Mantras
81. The Indian River Ganges
82. The Indian Architecture
83. Rites of Passage
84. The Indian Silk Road
85. The Indian Literature
86. The Indian Villages
87. The Indian Folks & Crafts
88. The Way of Buddha
89. The Ramayan of Tulsidas

90. Astrological Remedies
91. The Secret Power of Motivation
92. Secret of Developing your Inner Strength
93. The Secret Path to Motivation
94. The Art and Secret of Positive Thinking
95. The Secrets of Practicing Ethical Living
96. Indian Art and Painting
97. The Indian Herbalism
98. Bharatanatyam to Kathak
99. Exploring India's Astrological Remedies
100. The Indian Festival of Flowers
101. Indian Handicrafts
102. The Splashes of Joy – India's Colour Festival
103. The Indian Science of Astrology
104. The Indian Mythology
105. Path to Enlightenment
106. The Indian Spirituality for Children
107. Aromas of India
108. The Secrets of Healthy Relationships
109. Ancestral Ties
110. The Indian Street Food
111. Discovering America
112. The Indian Textile
113. Listening to Motivational Speeches
114. Taste of India
115. A Cultural Journey through Indian Nuptials
116. Motivational Quote for Change
117. Secret Strategies for Making Money
118. Secrets to Cultivate a Positive Mindset
119. A Tapestry of Cultures: Exploring India from Kashmir to Kanyakumari
120. Achieving Your Dreams with Resilience: Secret Strategies for Overcoming Obstacles

121. Innovative Startups - 25 Startup Ideas to Spark Your Business Creativity
122. Export Management: Strategies for Global Success
123. Exporting from India - A Step by Step Guide
124. Finance Fundamentals: Mastering Financial Management for Business Success
125. Global Growth Strategies for International Business Development
126. Marketing Mastery: Unlocking the Secrets of Modern Marketing
127. Operations Mastery: Managing the Flow of Value in Business
128. Strategic Business Management: Navigating the Modern Business Landscape
129. Human Resource Management Strategies for Building and Managing a High Performance Team
130. The Indian Landscapes and Nature: An Exploration Of India's Natural Beauty And Diversity
131. The Indian Street Performances: A Cultural Exploration of India's Street Performances
132. Affirming Your Self-Worth: Strategies for Achieving Emotional Wellbeing
133. Cultivating Self-Discipline: Secrets Methods for Achieving Your Goals
134. Embracing Change: Strategies for Adapting to Life's Challenges
135. Embracing Your Uniqueness: Secret Strategies for Living an Authentic Life
136. Finding Motivation in Despondency: Coping with Difficult Times
137. Embracing Change
138. Learning to Love Yourself
139. Managing Time for Yourself

140. Unlock the keys to Self-Motivation
141. Secret to Boost Confidence
142. Unlocking your Potential: A Path to Inner-strength & Success
143. Secrets to Develop Authentic Relationship
144. Secrets to Build a Successful Career
145. Secrets to Live with Gratitude
146. Secrets to Create a Life of Abundance
147. Secrets to Cultivate Self-Awareness
148. The Power of Helping Hands
149. Finding Your Passion
150. The Indian Mythical Creatures
151. The Indian Women Saints
152. The Wisdom of the Saints
153. "The Indian Royalty: A Cultural and Historical Exploration of India's Maharajas and their kingdom"
154. The Mystic Land: A Cultural and Spiritual Exploration of India"
155. India's Spiritual Legacy – Discovering the Cultural and Religious Significance of Bhakti Yoga.
156. The Indian Folktales: An Exploration of India's Oral Folklore Traditions
157. Steeping In History: A Look at India's Iconic Tea Culture
158. The Indian Way Of Life: An Exploration Of The Philosophy And Practices Of Indian Culture

CONTACT

DR. JAGADEESH PILLAI

MBA & PhD in Vedic Science

Four Times Guinness World Record Holder

Winner of Mahatma Gandhi Vishwa Shanti Puraskar and Global Peace Ambassador

Gemology, Astro & Vastu Consultant - Spiritual Counselor

Consultant for designing World Record Ideas

Efficient Tarot Card Reader

9839093003

myrichindia@gmail.com

drjagadeeshpillai@facebook

drjagadeeshpillai@instagram
jagadeeshpillai@youtube

www. JAGADEESHPILLAI.com

|| LOKAHA SAMASTHAHA SUKHINO BHAVANTU ||

ഇ

9 798889 595632

Printed by Libri Plureos GmbH in Hamburg, Germany